Classroom Crisis

"Dr. Johnson's book is an extremely practical guide for schools and student services providers in dealing with school crisis. Every guidance counselor, psychologist, and social worker in our district has been provided a copy of the book to assist them in schools when tragedy happens. In a district as large as ours, a unified approach to school crisis is essential.

Dr. Johnson is a leader in the field of trauma in children and provides very useful information for both the classroom teacher and others called to serve in a time of crisis. This book should be an essential part of any school crisis management plan."

— Carol Madura
Director, Drug-Free Schools Program
Pinellas County Office of Education, Florida

"*Dealing with Crisis in the Classroom* has been a valuable tool for teachers in the Long Beach Unified School District (LBUSD). On September 11, after the terrorist attacks on New York and Washington, DC, requests for the booklet began pouring into the central office from schools at every level. More than 1,000 booklets were put into LBUSD teachers' hands in those first hours alone. The booklet has been praised by teachers as being extremely user-friendly—the perfect tool to help children at the classroom level during and after crises. It is easy to understand and easy to use.

Kendall Johnson is one of the foremost international experts on the topic of school crisis response. He uses his tremendous grasp of the subject to transform complex ideas into a simple and understandable resource. *Dealing with Crisis in the Classroom* gives teachers thoughtful and practical answers to the question,

"But what do I do?" It also gives great guidelines for knowing when children need additional help. **If there is one book that a teacher needs for dealing with the unthinkable, this is it."**

— Joanne Tortorici Luna, Ph.D.
Professor of Educational Psychology
California State University, Long Beach
Crisis Team Leader, Long Beach Unified School District

This book is a must-read for anyone responsible for organizing a response to a school trauma. Kendall writes in easy-to-understand language about a complex subject, allowing the reader to draw upon the author's vast experience in this field.

Having trained hundreds of school personnel in Michigan around this subject, I heartily recommend this book as a very helpful aide in responding to children, faculty, and the community when terrible things happen in our school."

— Dennis Potter, MSW, FAAETS
Kantu Consultants and
Clinical Director, Mid-West Michigan Crisis Response Team

"Seldom does a practitioner in the area of trauma resolution speak to the heart and soul of healing as Kendall Johnson has done with his new book. This contribution to the literature is easy to read, and the vivid examples illuminate the often dark recesses of resolving loss, grief, and trauma.

After my professional efforts at the Pentagon on 9-11 involving significant exposure and fatigue, who was I going to turn to? Kendall became my support and debriefer—the traumatologist healer! It is because of his depth of caring, creativity, and scholarship that many persons have been assisted in dealing with the life-changing, charged, and churning challenges that loss/grief and trauma bring."

— Victoria Bruner, LCSW
Walter Reed Army Medical Center

About the Author

Kendall Johnson, Ph.D., serves as a crisis-management consultant to several major school districts nationwide and teaches in the Claremont Unified School District. He is a twenty-five-year veteran classroom teacher, is NBPTS board certified in adolescent/young adult art, and has served as a mentor teacher. In addition, he is a licensed marriage and family therapist specializing in posttrauma issues and has trained school crisis-response teams for seventeen years. Dr. Johnson serves in an advisory capacity to the Psychological Trauma Center, Los Angeles; Harlem Hospital, New York City; Walter Reed Army Medical Center, Washington D.C.; and Mercy Corps. He serves on the faculty of the International Critical Incident Stress Foundation and on the editorial board of the *International Journal of Emergency Mental Health*. In addition to journal articles and training materials, Dr. Johnson has written the books *Trauma in the Lives of Children; Responding to School Crisis: A CISM Approach;* and *School Crisis Management*. He is currently completing a book titled *After the Storm: Healing after Trauma, Tragedy and Terror* (forthcoming in 2004 from Hunter House Publishers).

Dedication

These are perilous times in general, even more so in the class-room. This book is dedicated to those who endure anyway, prompted by their love of their profession and sense of duty to those they serve.

Classroom Crisis THE TEACHER'S GUIDE

Kendall Johnson, Ph.D.

Hunter House
PUBLISHERS

Library of Congress Cataloging-in-Publication Data
Johnson, Kendall, 1945-
    Classroom crisis : the teacher's guide / Kendall Johnson.— 2nd ed.
    p. cm.
Includes bibliographical references (p.   ) and index.
    ISBN-13: 978-0-89793-432-9 (pbk.)
    ISBN-10: 0-89793-432-6 (pbk.)
    1. School crisis management—United States—Handbooks, manuals, etc.
2. Crisis intervention (Mental health services)—United States—Handbooks, manuals, etc. 3. School psychology—United States—Handbooks, manuals, etc. I. Title.
LB2866.5.J63 2004
371.7'13—dc22   2003023961

Project Credits
Cover Design: Jinni Fontana Graphic Design
Book Design and Production: Jinni Fontana Graphic Design
Copy Editor: Kelley Blewster
Proofreader: Lee Rappold
Acquisitions Editor: Jeanne Brondino
Editor: Alexandra Mummery
Publicist: Lisa E. Lee
Foreign Rights Assistant: Elisabeth Wohofsky
Customer Service Manager: Christina Sverdrup
Order Fulfillment: Washul Lakdhon
Administrator: Theresa Nelson
Computer Support: Peter Eichelberger
Publisher: Kiran S. Rana

Manufactured in the United States of America

9 8 7 6 5 4   Second Edition   12 13 14 15 16

Contents

Foreword. ix

Introduction 1

1 | What Are Critical Incidents?. 3

2 | Managing Behavior During Emergencies 6

3 | Group Management During Emergencies. 17

4 | What's Normal Following Crisis?. 19

5 | Typical Postcrisis Behavior. 22

6 | Serious Signs. 27

7 | Individual Conferencing about Crisis. 30

8 | Classroom Discussions 33

9 | Group and Classroom Interventions 37

10 | Talking with Children about War, Terror, and Disaster 39

11 | What *Not* to Do 41

12 | Dealing with Distraught Parents 43

13 | Understanding Administrator Stress 46

14 | Your Own Reaction 48

15 | Self-Care. 51

Resources 61

Warning/Disclaimer

This guide is intended to be used by school staff members in pursuit of their normal duties in unusual situations. It is by no means intended to train individuals to be psychotherapists, but rather to simply do their existing jobs in a more effective manner. Further, it is in no way intended to substitute for qualified psychological therapy or consultation. Readers are advised to utilize all available help from district psychologists and administrators or from outside district-approved sources when dealing with classroom crisis. Further, this guide makes no attempt to address legal issues of responsibility or liability for educators.

The material in this book is intended to provide a review of information regarding how to manage crisis in the classroom. Every effort has been made to provide accurate and dependable information. The contents of this book have been compiled through professional research and in consultation with mental-health and medical professionals. However, mental-health professionals have differing opinions, and advances in medical and scientific research are made very quickly, so some of the information may become outdated.

Therefore, the publisher, author, and editors, and the professionals quoted in the book cannot be held responsible for any error, omission, or dated material. The author and publisher assume no responsibility for any outcome of applying the information in this book in a program of self-care or under the care of a licensed practitioner. If you have questions concerning the application of the information described in this book, consult a qualified mental-health professional and your building administrator.

Foreword

In 1990, as a newly assigned Director of Pupil Personnel Services for a large Manhattan school district, I watched the evening news with one eye closed and prayed during each story involving children, "Please let this not be one of my schools." Although a novice, I was knowledgeable enough to know that the closed-eye method was insufficient for the role I might need to play.

Fortunately for the district's forty schools, I attended a training session with Dr. Kendall Johnson on school crisis response. Subsequently, we enlisted his help in the training of all the district's school counselors and set up a district-level crisis team. The knowledge and expertise we gained as a group sustained our schools through ten years of critical incidents of varying degrees, from a school-bus accident to the deaths of students, parents, and faculty, including the sudden death of a principal.

Then, there was September 11, 2001! Four of our schools lay in the shadow of the World Trade Center and were evacuated in smoke and darkness, surrounded by crowds of running adults. Another thirty-six schools were located within four miles of the attack site. The enormity of the disaster was overwhelming and unlike any of the hundreds of crisis events we'd previously encountered.

How does one make sense of the unimaginable, the unthinkable? With adults grappling for understanding and all of humanity glued to the television watching the ongoing horrific images, how does a teacher lead, guide, explain, and comfort? For New Yorkers, the images were not on the TV set, but on the streets. The sights, the sounds, the smells were terrifying and unnerving.

Children craved comfort, teachers and principals required support, and parents needed guidance. There were not (and could never be) enough crisis-team members to be all things to all schools, and district staff members were running on empty. Under such critical circumstances children turn to the person whom they know and trust—the classroom teacher. For this reason all efforts must be expended to help you, the teacher, be more knowledgeable and skilled, and thus more comfortable, in the role you may be compelled to take.

One person's hindsight can be helpful to others. Looking back, what have I learned? I know that all schools need training. I know that all teachers are on the front line and need a basic tool kit. I know that Dr. Johnson's book offers the sage, simple, and practical advice that would have been beneficial to all our teachers.

We in New York live with a "new normal." The support of those around the country truly helped us through the aftermath of September 11. We are grateful to the teachers across the country who sent banners, bears, cards, and comfort. And a special personal thanks goes to Ken Johnson for his help to us, and for what he is offering to educators in this book. Dr. Johnson appeared in New York in November 2001, when we were all nearing exhaustion. His calm demeanor, wisdom, and expertise gave us renewed energy, hope, and a sense that we could accomplish the challenges that lay before us. We, the beneficiaries of his gentle guidance, will remain forever grateful.

It is our sincere hope that all teachers and school administrators on the front lines will use *Classroom Crisis: The Teacher's Guide* to help keep their eyes wide open and to gain the essential information and tools they need to knowledgeably care for those in their charge.

— Marjorie S. Robbins, Director
9/11 School Recovery Program
Consultant, CSD 2, NYC Department of Education

Introduction

On the morning of January 28, 1986, children in classrooms across the country viewed televised coverage of the launching of the space shuttle *Challenger* as part of their curriculum. They watched in silence as the shuttle exploded just after liftoff, killing its crew of seven, including a classroom teacher. As the initial moments of shock gave way to the realization of what had actually happened, tens of thousands of teachers, specially trained or not, were faced with the task of dealing with their students who were stunned, shaken, and deeply upset over what they had just witnessed. Some teachers, not knowing what else to do, turned off the set and resumed normal class routine. Barely able to cope with the incident themselves, they hoped that someone else could help their students sort things out.

A version of the material in this book was originally prepared at that time to help teachers and other school professionals deal with incidents that present new and overwhelming challenges to schools. Since then, the techniques of school crisis management have continued to evolve, and this book has been updated to reflect those changes.

Since 1986 the school setting has become more volatile. Suicide attempts, assaults, shootings—even mass murders—have turned school campuses from sanctuaries to crime scenes. Recently, a series of unthinkable events has underscored the need for crisis preparedness in schools. To mention the following cities evokes memories of mayhem on an unprecedented scale: Littleton, El Cajon, and Lower Manhattan. We can no longer assume that the school year will pass uneventfully. Nor can we assume that our children will avoid being directly impacted by acts of terrorism or madness.

School staff members need material and training that deal with how to manage students during and following crisis events. This booklet is intended to provide such tools in a usable format. Specific guidelines are presented that give teachers direction in handling students' emergency behavior and providing follow-up support.

It would be nice if this material were not necessary.

1

What Are Critical Incidents?

Critical incidents are events that overwhelm an individual's capacity to cope and that negatively affect classroom behavior and climate. They can be psychologically traumatic, causing emotional turmoil, cognitive problems, learning difficulties, and behavioral changes. The effects of a critical incident can be lasting, depending upon individual resiliency as well as the quality of the person's experiences during and shortly after the incident. The degree and rate of recovery of a person affected by crisis is determined in part by how much he or she is surrounded by supportive, caring people who help him or her deal with the aftermath of the experience. Actions taken by school personnel can help restore individual and classroom stability.

The recent siege of school shootings, bombings, civil disorder, terrorist attacks, and gang violence bear testimony to the possibility of large-scale, dramatic trauma. The victimization or death of a classmate, an attempted suicide of a friend, or a shocking event witnessed by a group happen far more frequently in the lives of schoolchildren than was the case even just a decade ago. Because the classroom is not insulated from the world at large, events that take place in the classroom often occur in response to events in the world.

Some frequently asked questions about critical incidents are:

How often do they happen in a classroom?

It is quite likely that any given class will experience one or possibly several critical incidents in a year.

How do they affect a class?

An event that happens to one child affects other classmates vicariously. A class is an intimate group, and just as experiences of individual family members affect the rest of the family, one student's experiences will affect the rest of the class. Shared difficulties can bring classes together or pull them apart, affecting class climate, behavior, and performance.

What is "acute stress response"?

Most students will be upset by extreme events, but will remain functional and able to respond to your leadership. Some may be overwhelmed. Of those who are overwhelmed, some will overreact (become agitated) and some will underreact (shut down). These reactions are both forms of *acute stress response* (ASR), and they both create temporary problems in students' thinking, feeling, and behavior.

What is "delayed stress response"?

Sometimes the effects of a crisis do not surface until weeks, months, or even years later. This is called *delayed stress response*. It is thought that delayed stress response happens when the strategies used to cope with the critical incident prohibit the emotional processing of the event. Later, as the individual attempts to adapt to the changed circumstances, memories and feelings about the incident emerge, causing distress and further attempts to cope. Both temporary problems at the time of the crisis and delayed problems can later escalate into serious disorders such as anxiety or depressive syndromes, dissociation, or even posttraumatic stress disorder.

Why must I become involved?

For two reasons. First, studies have shown that the way in which an adult responds to individuals and groups following crisis can significantly affect the outcome of that experience. Through effective, caring intervention, negative acute and delayed stress responses can be minimized. Second, the process of effectively intervening with individuals or groups is a tremendous group builder and can create a sense of cohesiveness and belonging in a classroom.

Can crisis affect learning?

Crisis does affect learning by creating instability in the life of the classroom and in the life of the student. Trauma alters brain chemistry and function, causing students to have difficulty in concentration, memory, and behavior. Further, the classroom climate and process can be altered in a way that sabotages the learning environment.

Can the district help me to help my class?

Yes. School districts have various resources available. Your district may have a crisis team in place, and your school may have one also. Crisis teams can consist of school psychologists, counselors, teachers, or outside resource personnel who can provide consultation and direct assistance. They may be available to consult with students you refer for assessment and support, they may be available to help you address crisis needs in your class, or they may be available to answer questions and suggest strategies for you. Begin by discussing the situation with your building principal and other teachers.

2

Managing Behavior During Emergencies

Emergency situations create intense stress that can affect student behavior—individual and group. Examples of such incidents can include:

♦ A student's extreme personal crisis

♦ Crisis events at school or in the community

♦ Natural disaster

♦ Shooter or bomb on campus

♦ Confinement in classroom during lockdown

♦ Exposure to another person's injuries

♦ Evacuation from classroom or school

You can manage most students who have extreme reactions to events like these, but there are a few things you need to know. You need to know how to size up students' response levels, how to identify the two general response patterns to extreme stress, and how to implement the approach strategies for managing each. You then need to know how to handle the group when some class members are reacting poorly. Finally, you need to know how to support students afterward. Fortunately, these tasks are fairly simple and straightforward.

Levels of Response

When bad things happen, we respond. Our response includes our thoughts, feelings, and actions. Response levels to any situation range from mild to extreme. Acute stress reactions fall on both extremes of the behavioral spectrum; that is, they can be described as either extremely shut down or extremely agitated.

Note that I use the word *extreme* to describe acute stress reactions. By their very definition, reactions that fall under the ASR (acute stress response) umbrella aren't moderate. Note also that I refer to a *spectrum* of possible responses to crisis. That spectrum is centered in normal, fully present awareness. Full awareness is what we experience when we walk into a room with the intention of seeing what's there, or when we listen intently to what another person is saying. In such a state of awareness, we are open to new information. From such a state of awareness, our response level can extend either way: toward greater engagement with the situation on the one hand, or toward less engagement on the other.

It is useful to divide the spectrum of response to crisis into seven degrees. Notice that item four, "fully present," falls right in the middle of the scale:

1. Acute stress shutdown

2. Faded

3. Objective

4. Fully present

5. Involved

6. Overreactive

7. Acute stress agitation

The table on page 8 describes each of these degrees of response in more detail.

Position on spectrum	Description
Acute stress shutdown	Unable to respond
Faded	Becoming disconnected from the situation and from one's own reactions
Objective	Personal involvement is secondary to an overall perspective
Present	Fully aware and focused on the situation
Involved	Some degree of personal involvement and subjectivity
Overreactive	Personal involvement overrides a broader perspective
Acute stress agitation	Unable to control or direct behavior

Acute Stress Reactions

Again, the two response extremes are *shutdown* and *agitation*. They look very different:

Shutdown	Agitation
Pale, shocklike appearance	Flushed, sweaty appearance
Submissive	Panic, enraged, or hysterical affect
Blunted affect, slowed behavior	Rapid, undirected, ineffective action
Extreme: paralysis, immobility	Extreme: uncontrolled

If you recognize any of these reactions in a student, it may be wise to intervene to help stabilize him or her. This is because in order to stabilize a situation, you must first stabilize the individuals involved. Each of the two forms of ASR can be handled, but they must be dealt with differently.

But before we look at different ways to intervene in the two respective forms of ASR, let's consider the general principles that apply to dealing with *both* forms of ASR. *First*, they must each be dealt with at the levels of thought, emotion, bodily actions, and behavior. *Second*, the goals for intervening at each of these levels is the same, whether the reaction is one of shutdown or agitation. See the table below for a summary of the goals of intervention in ASR.

Managing ASR: Intervention Levels and Goals	
Level	**Goal**
Thoughts	Focus attention
Feelings	Stabilize feelings
Body	Adjust pacing
Behavior	Direct action

Third, because our thoughts—what we think about a situation and how we frame it in our mind—are easier to change than our emotions, physical reactions, or behavior, when intervening in a person's response to crisis, it is helpful to start by offering strategies for changing his or her thoughts. In particular, you should attempt to shift the person's focus, self-talk, and mental images. (More about each of these suggestions is included below.) Then proceed to dealing with emotions, physical reactions, and behavior, respectively. The tools offered below are presented in that order.

Tools for Dealing with Reactions to Crisis

Use the following tools—in roughly the order in which they are presented here—to manage extreme behavior so you can keep control of your class and stabilize the situation. *Be aware that the tools are used in a different way to deal with students who are agitated than with those who are shutting down.*

No matter which tool or tools you use, the way you approach students in the midst of crisis affects their behavior. It is important to stay calm and positive.

◇ Focus

Imagination can fire fears. Work at keeping students focused on the here and now. If a student is shutting down, direct his or her attention outward. If he or she is growing agitated, shift his or her attention back to himself or herself.

◇ Self-Talk/Other Talk

The words we choose to describe crisis events shape our expectation regarding what is going to happen, and those expectations in turn guide their reactions. Use clear language when talking to students. Don't use extreme or evocative words when normal words will do. Speak in calming ways. Use reminders like "Let's stop and think this through"; "Things will work out"; "Stay focused and stay strong."

◇ Imagery

Mental pictures guide our actions and our response. Mental pictures can be used to calm ourselves down or push us into action.

They can be directly suggested or simply embedded in conversation. Tell your students to visualize positive outcomes.

◇ Feelings

Feelings can strongly influence both physical reactions and thought processes. These responses can be intensified (in the case of shutdown) or softened (in the case of agitation) by words and images. Also, alternative sets of feelings can be elicited by directing attention to different aspects of the situation. Use a calming tone of voice, body posture, and facial expression. Look the person in the eye and hold their gaze. Stand right in front of them as you speak. Tell them what you see happening in order to redirect their attention.

◇ Breath

By changing a person's breathing patterns, both their thoughts and physical reactions can also be changed. To lower the level of reaction in cases of agitation, teach students "four-count breathing": Inhale deeply for a slow count of four. Then hold the breath for another four count. Next, release the breath slowly over a count of four. Then hold it out for a count of four. Repeat the process four times. This breathing technique initiates the relaxation response.

Alternatively, to escalate a student's reactions in the case of shutdown, simply have him or her take several panting breaths quickly ("quick breaths"). This technique initiates the arousal response.

◇ Bodily Pacing

To focus thoughts and control feelings, direct students to intentionally slow down their body movements. Alternatively, if you want to help a student mobilize thoughts and get in touch with feelings, direct him or her to pick up the pacing of movements.

◈ Directing Physical Energy

During agitation, the body is jerky and hyperactive. Redirecting body energy to more deliberate, productive tasks allows that energy to dissipate. During shutdown, the body is inert, awaiting direction and conserving energy. Stretching, moving around, and taking purposive action allows the energy to flow again. Ask a student who is shutting down or agitating to accompany you while you do things. Walk, move, and speak at a pace similar to the student's, then gradually slow down if he or she is agitated, or speed up if he or she is fading. When the student is responding favorably, give her or him an appropriate task to complete.

◈ Action

Give students something to do. This will help to either elevate or calm down their reaction levels and redirect their attention more meaningfully. Some suggested actions are simple: "Take a walk" or "Sit down." Others are more complex: "Take this box to that person." "Organize these papers." "Please pack these lunches." The purpose of the action is twofold: to appropriately direct energy and focus, and to reestablish a sense of control and self-worth. Activities must be within the range of the student's ability at the time.

◈ Ritual

Everyday rituals can increase people's awareness, help them balance their emotions, and focus their energy. Some rituals mobilize people's energy to face challenges. Sports teams, for instance, sometimes have everyone touch hands together and yell their team name before a game. A teacher might have all the students take a deep breath together or sing a brief song. Even just having "everyone put their work away" reinforces a sense of normalcy. Having students do a "quickwrite" before having a serious discussion can also help normalize the moment. Other rituals can bring comfort and a sense of community support. A brief moment of silence together or holding hands in a circle followed by everyone taking one step inward can remind students that the group has cohesiveness. Intentionally use your existing classroom patterns and routines as rituals during stressful times.

The extreme reactions of agitation and shutdown are discussed below; then group management and support are considered.

Dealing with Agitation

When those around us become agitated, they represent a risk to themselves and others.

Look for:

- ◆ Overreacting
- ◆ Catastrophic thinking
- ◆ Panic, rage, hysteria
- ◆ Rapid breathing, sweating
- ◆ Agitated, frantic, and unproductive behavior

Your goals are to:

- ◆ Refocus the student's attention inward.
- ◆ Help the student shift his or her expectations.

- Attend to the present moment.
- Help the student lower his or her oxygen and adrenaline levels.
- Initiate the relaxation response.
- Guide the student to lower his or her activity level.
- Redirect his or her activity toward something useful.

To implement these goals, try the following (for more detail, see "Tools for Dealing with Reactions to Crisis," starting on page 10):

- Use a soothing and calming tone; encourage talking.
- Use neutral descriptions; suggest positive outcomes/images.
- Use distracting talk and actions.
- Initiate and lead four-count breathing.
- Sit the student down; change his or her location; model relaxation.
- Help the student stretch; take a walk; do things slowly.
- Give the student something useful to do.

USE CARE IN APPROACHING SOMEONE WHO SHOWS SIGNS OF PANIC, HYSTERIA, OR RAGE.

Keep enough distance at first.

Do not grab the person.

Use gestures that are reassuring.

Make sure your voice tone is nonconfrontational.

Dealing with Shutdown

When those around us shut down, they cannot help themselves and are at increased risk for delayed stress reactions.

Look for:

- Little responsiveness
- Vacant expression
- Little emotion
- Lack of muscle tone
- Immobile or slowed pace and movement

Your goals are to:

- Refocus the student's attention outward.
- Help the student shift her or his expectations.
- Help the student broaden his or her perspective.
- Help him or her raise oxygen and adrenaline levels.
- Initiate the arousal response.
- Increase the student's activity level.

To implement these goals, try the following (for more detail, see "Tools for Dealing with Reactions to Crisis," starting on page 10):

- Help the student take several quick breaths.
- Suggest and help the student visualize actions.
- Provide simple directions.
- Use an empowering, encouraging tone and touch.
- Suggest and demonstrate faster breathing and bodily movements.

- Help the student walk around or move rapidly.
- Give the student things to do.

**REMEMBER, WITH EITHER AGITATED OR
SHUTDOWN ACUTE STRESS RESPONSE (ASR):**

Do not leave anyone alone who's suffering from ASR;

Get medical help as soon as possible.

3

mm

Group Management During Emergencies

Handling a class during an emergency requires stronger leadership and clearer direction than during normal times. Your job is to keep the children safe; in part, this means managing their reactions so you can maintain order. It is especially important to avoid contagion—that is, when one student's extreme behavior begins triggering others—as much as possible. Here are some steps for managing a group during emergencies. As before, these are listed in roughly the order in which they should be followed.

- ◆ Take a strong leadership role.
- ◆ Remember that management of the group takes priority.
- ◆ Separate and contain dysfunctional individuals.
- ◆ Focus the main group on a task.
- ◆ Deal with dysfunctional members individually, if possible.
- ◆ If possible, utilize peer support from the least difficult group.
- ◆ Reintegrate dysfunctional students when possible; keep separate if not.

If time allows, provide support to individuals and to the group as a whole:

♦ If the situation allows, engage the group in conversation. This helps reestablish a sense of normalcy and control.

♦ Ask what they understand about what's happening.

♦ Try to acknowledge and clarify class members' thoughts and feelings.

♦ Show them through your words and actions that you are trying to help.

♦ Avoid contradicting their feelings or making false assurances.

♦ Use active listening. Repeat back what they tell you in order to show them that you listened carefully. Check out whether you understood correctly by asking, "Is that what you mean?"

♦ If you think someone's misunderstanding of the situation is making things worse, provide a clearer picture in words they will understand.

♦ If you feel that someone is beginning to fade, help to refocus them using the techniques described above. Similarly, if they are fearful or overly excited, help them relax.

♦ If in group or class, monitor disclosure. Remember, the students must live with the social consequences of disclosing things that may be used against them later by the group.

Let them know what's going to happen next, as far as you know it.

Look for signs of distress.

4

~mm~

What's Normal
Following Crisis?

In dealing with children following a critical incident, it is useful to know what to expect. Adjustment behavior is different from everyday, regular behavior, because a great deal of inner work is going on in the process of assimilating the experience. Teachers need to have some sense of what is and is not "normal" during this unusual time.

In order to cope with the extreme stress of critical incidents, those affected frequently suppress certain thoughts and feelings. This coping process allows the individual to do what must be done to maintain psychological and physical equilibrium. These crisis experiences, too threatening and disturbing to be assimilated at once, may gradually surface later to be fully integrated. This is a natural process of self-healing.

Crisis involves change. More than just a simple emotional process, crisis experiences force the child to accommodate new, discrepant, and frequently threatening information about the world. The sudden realizations crisis brings—of vulnerability, loss of support of loved ones, or large-scale rejection—are all difficult to get used to.

As the child attempts to accommodate this new information cognitively, the thoughts and feelings associated with the incident begin to surface. The child may reexperience fear, anger, or help-lessness. As the child begins to experience the new changes in his or her life, anxiety, fear, shame, guilt, and depression may follow. The emotional reactions to this process can themselves be a fright-ening, stressful, and out-of-control experience.

In managing the student (or the class) who is recovering from crisis, several points are worth remembering:

- **Normalcy.** Emotional upset and faltering attempts to work out coping systems following a crisis are not indications of mental illness. Rather, they are very normal reactions to abnormal circumstances. To classify such a person as crazy and assume that only psychologists are qualified to talk to him simply deprives that individual of much needed support and healthy interaction.

- **Instability.** Critical incidents alone, even the most severe, do not cause mental illness in the vast majority of cases. Preex-isting mental instability, however, may be reactivated by extreme stress. See the later section titled "Serious Signs" for further discussion regarding signs of more serious insta-bility.

- **Epicycles.** Normal recovery can be a long process, and prob-ably will include times that appear as though the child is get-ting worse rather than better. Again, this is normal and quite likely a part of the natural healing process. As the child becomes stronger, she is able to deal with more intrusive memories, thoughts, and feelings. Reactions to these intru-sive images can strain newly developed coping skills.

- **Ages and stages.** Often, years of relative calm go by without difficulty, and it seems that the crisis is really over. Then, suddenly, new problems arise. Normal developmental transitions create new realities, and these changes make previously successful coping strategies obsolete. As short-term coping skills become outworn, new ones must be developed. Until they are, painful memories are more intrusive and more difficult. Often, during these transitional times, regressive or maladaptive behavior develops as a misguided attempt at coping. Adolescence, in particular, is likely to foster maladaptive attempt at adjustment. The next section, "Typical Postcrisis Behavior," offers more about what to expect from children at various ages.

5

mm

Typical
Postcrisis Behavior

Everyone's response to critical incidents is unique. Yet each of us shows a change in our behavior as a response to crisis, and those changes frequently fall into patterns. Children are no different, although their patterns are limited by their particular stage of development and personal history.

The following descriptions of typical posttraumatic behavior patterns may be useful for you in observing your students. Consider them as signs of possible prior trauma; or, if you know that a critical incident has occurred, consider them as likely responses to serious crisis. Notice that each progressive age may involve behaviors from earlier developmental levels.

*Among **preschool** or **kindergarten-age** children:*

+ **Withdrawal.** Children may become unusually quiet and seemingly detached from others. They may act subdued and possibly even become mute with adults or peers.

+ **Denial.** Denial may take many forms, including denial of facts and memories of events, avoidance of certain themes or issues in play or discussion, and ignoring certain people or conditions.

- **Thematic play.** This encompasses frequent participation in reenactments or ritualistic play that follows a theme of either the trauma itself or life upsets that are secondary to the trauma (such as family problems or circumstantial changes).

- **Anxious attachment.** Such behavior includes greater separation and stranger anxiety. Clinging, whining, refusing to let go of parents or favorite objects, and having tantrums are frequently observed signs. Since such behavior often also occurs under normal circumstances during this developmental stage, look for changes in frequency, duration, and intensity.

- **Specific fears.** Some common specific fears can include fear of new situations, strangers, males, confinement, violence, or certain objects.

- **Regression.** Under severe stress, children attempt to master the situation by reverting to behavior patterns they found successful at earlier developmental stages. This represents a search for a comfort zone.

*Among **school-age** children, any of the above behaviors, plus:*

- **Performance decline.** A decline in performance in one or several areas may indicate a posttraumatic reaction among school-age children. School and intellectual performance, sports, music lessons, and other hobbies could all be affected.

- **Compensatory behavior.** Behavior designed to compensate for the critical incident or its resulting loss, injury, or unwanted changes may be evident. Such behaviors may be attempts to deny, reverse, or gain retribution through fantasy, play, or interaction.

♦ **Obsessive talking.** Once the child feels free to talk about the incident, he or she may talk about it continually. This is a necessary part of the process of assimilating the event and will likely be temporary.

♦ **Discrepancy in mood.** The child may express feelings or moods that seem inappropriate to the immediate situation or to the events he or she is describing. Sometimes this represents an attempt to avoid full realization, and other times it is the result of the child's preoccupation with past events.

♦ **Behavior changes or problems.** These may include getting in trouble, sudden changes in interest, or regressive behavior. Often these behaviors result from attempts to relieve anxiety, gain needed attention, or sort through new, troubling information about the world or the child him- or herself.

♦ **More elaborate enactments.** Reenactments become progressively more sophisticated, although often no more satisfactory than during early childhood.

♦ **Psychosomatic complaints.** Stomachaches, headaches, digestive upsets, etc., are often very real symptoms of psychological distress. Sometimes they are thinly disguised bids for extra time and attention. Such complaints are often indirect communications about other things.

*Among **adolescents,** any of the above behaviors, plus:*

♦ **Acting-out behavior.** Perhaps because of a combination of peer influence and a need not to defer to parental support, adolescents often act out their distress in ways that are ultimately self-destructive. These can include isolation, truancy, drug and alcohol abuse, sexual activity, violence, delinquency, running away, or suicidal expression or attempts.

- **Low self-esteem and self-criticism.** Adolescents are quick to blame themselves and to condemn their own reactions to crisis situations. They often have fanciful expectations regarding their control over situations, and anything going wrong is interpreted as a blow to their sense of power and independence.

- **Acting too old too fast.** This behavior is often seen among poverty-stricken children who must compete in the streets with adults, and among child prodigies who must deal with adults constantly. Likewise, traumatized adolescents sometimes develop lifestyles several years in advance of their chronological age.

- **Displaced anger.** Because you may be the safest person the adolescent confronts during the day, you may be the unwilling and undeserving recipient of anger that has no other place to go.

- **Preoccupation with self.** Trauma, and the resulting inner processing that must be done to sort through the meaning of the incident, can intensify the adolescent's normal self-centeredness.

The above signs of crisis are serious and indicate the need for medical or psychological assessment. They may represent a serious psychological condition. Share your observations with your principal or site administrator, health or guidance personnel, and the child's parent. These behaviors also may represent a serious stressor outside of school. If you suspect there may be child abuse, you are probably mandated to report your suspicions and observations to police and/or child protective services. Learn what the procedure is for your educational agency, learn what your legal responsibilities are, and respond in a timely manner. You may be liable if you don't.

IF YOU NOTICE UNUSUAL BEHAVIOR, START EXPLORING FOR THE "WHY?"

Ask gentle, general questions.

Look for corroborating behavior.

Be prepared to pursue the issue.

6

mm

Serious Signs

The preceding section describes normal recovery patterns. Sometimes a student's behavior following a critical incident goes to greater extremes, warranting immediate referral to mental-health specialists. Your school has established procedures for determining when and how such a referral is to be made. Consult with your principal if you have any questions about the appropriateness of the procedure or referral. In general, when in doubt, find out.

The following guidelines are an attempt to sharpen your perceptions about when a referral of a student to a school counselor or psychologist is a consideration. ***The guidelines are NOT intended to serve as a checklist to be used in ruling out a referral!*** These signs are serious, and many lesser signs warrant further investigation. If you have concerns, follow them up. As always, discuss situations in which you feel uncomfortable or over your head with your school administrator, school psychologist or counselor, or health specialist.

The main difference between normal and serious reactions is one of degree more than kind. Serious reactions are simply normal reactions taken to extreme. Referral for normal reactions may be very helpful and should also be considered. Serious reactions, however, call for immediate referral.

The following descriptions may be helpful in distinguishing between normal and serious reactions. Reactions fall into three areas: cognitive, emotional, and behavioral.

Cognitive Signs

A cognitive reaction may be said to be serious when:

- Slight disorientation has become an inability to tell one's own name or the date, or to relate what has happened over the past twenty-four hours.

- Too much concern over little things has become an exclusive preoccupation with one idea.

- Denial of the severity of the problem has become a wholesale denial that an event or problem exists.

- Brief visual or auditory flashbacks have become hallucinations that are out of control.

- Self-doubt or feelings of unreality have become a fear of "losing one's mind" or an inability to stay in the present.

- Difficulty in planning practical things has become an inability to carry out basic life functions.

- Confusion has given way to bizarre, irrational beliefs, and such beliefs form the basis for action.

Emotional Signs

An emotional reaction may be said to be serious when:

- Crying has become uncontrolled hysteria.

- Anger or self-blame has become fear of or threats of harm to self or others.

- Blunted emotional response or numbing has become complete withdrawal with no emotional response.

- Appropriate expression of despair or depression has become self-destructive.

Behavioral Signs

A behavioral reaction may be said to be serious when:

- Restlessness or excitement has become unfocused agitation.

- Excessive talking or nervousness has become uncontrolled.

- Frequent retelling of the incident has become continual or ritualistic.

- Pacing, hand-wringing, or clenched fists have become ritualistic or uncontrolled.

- Withdrawal has become immobility or rigidity.

- Disheveled appearance over time becomes inability to care for oneself.

- Irritability has become destructive or assaultive.

Again, the above signs—as well as signs of acute stress response—indicate that, if conditions permit, the student should be referred immediately for medical or psychological evaluation. Review the signs of acute stress response outlined in the earlier section "Managing Behavior During Emergencies."

7

Individual Conferencing about Crisis

Individual conferencing can occur in several situations. A student may mention an important situation in a class discussion or writing assignment, and the teacher wishes to inquire further. A student may ask to speak privately and to take the teacher into his or her confidence. A student's performance or behavior alerts the teacher to a possible incident. Or perhaps the teacher hears a disquieting rumor and wishes to provide the right context in case the student chooses to talk.

The following strategies have proven helpful for individual conferences with students in distress:

- **Find privacy.** If possible, find a comfortable, private place for the conference. If the conference is to be one on one, it must be private in order to engage the student's trust. A word of caution, however: Avoid placing yourself in a compromising position, particularly if you are male with a female student. Stay visible to others.

- **Maintain calm.** In all probability, the student is experiencing uncertainty and self-doubt. Presenting a balanced demeanor tells the student that what he or she is about to say will be accepted.

- **Be honest with yourself.** Keep in touch with your own feelings and with your reaction to the student, the issues, and the situation. If you feel you cannot handle the situation, ask someone else to take over and then help arrange the transition.

- **Read between the lines.** Watch the student's behavior. Be aware of subtle messages. Draw inferences for further exploration.

- **Validate feelings.** Feelings are neither right nor wrong. Whatever feelings the student is expressing, validate them. Often lots of feelings clamor for expression; help the student to clarify them, and you will both watch them change. Try naming the feeling and asking whether it fits. If it doesn't, try another. Help the young person find the right words.

- **Listen well.** Good listening involves several skills. Use gentle probes for clarification and elaboration. Maintain good eye contact. Use increasingly focused questions when appropriate (especially when you suspect harm has been done to your student or to someone else). Trust your hunches and check them out.

- **Show belief.** Your job at this point is to listen and to facilitate expression. You are not a judge, jury, or investigator. Show confidence, trust, and faith that what the student is saying is the truth as he or she sees it.

- **Dispel fault.** If the student was victimized, let him or her know that the incident was not his or her fault. Be proactive about this, as victims tend to distrust and blame themselves.

- **Explore fears.** Young people often can talk about what happened to them, but may be unable to express their assumptions, questions, or fears about the incident.

Facilitating the expression of these assumptions, questions, and fears empowers the individual to deal with them.

♦ **Provide information.** The right information at the right time can be very helpful. If you know something about the incident, about normal reactions to that kind of incident, or about actions that could be taken, consider sharing it. Be sure not to preach, however, and be sure that your own need to "do something" is not clouding your judgment regarding the timeliness of the information.

♦ **Walk through the process.** Young people want to know what's going to happen next. There are many processes that are predictable, given a particular situation. Loss of a significant person will predictably involve the grief process. Disclosure of criminal victimization will predictably involve contacting the police and participating in other legal procedures. When the time is right, sharing what you know about certain processes can assist the student in predicting and planning for the future.

♦ **Explore resources.** As soon as possible, explore with the student what resources are available and what his or her support system provides. Assist the student in deciding to whom, when, and how they should reach out for that support.

♦ **Reestablish routine.** Get the students back into their normal classroom routine as quickly as possible. This sends a powerful message to them that the emergency is being controlled and that they are safe.

KEY ACTIONS

Validate feelings. *Facilitate expression.*

Explore resources. *Reestablish routine.*

8

~~~~

Classroom
Discussions

Group discussions are the simplest and most natural group intervention following a crisis. Teachers are usually the best qualified to conduct such discussions with their students. In general, they should follow guidelines similar to those for individual conferencing, taking into account the social dimensions of the situation.

Red Flags

Students can be vulnerable to harassment following group discussions if they disclose sensitive information to an unappreciative audience. Their well-being must be protected. Several "red flags" indicate when group discussion of an incident or other types of group interventions may be harmful.

◇ Group Red Flags

In general, think twice before using large group interventions with groups that demonstrate the following:

- Unsupportive climate
- Polarized needs

♦ Politicized and contentious attitudes and/or behavior

♦ Families greatly impacted by the incident

◇ Individual Red Flags

In addition, individual class members should not be included in group discussions regarding critical incidents if they exhibit the following signs of distress:

♦ Unfocused agitation

♦ Disconnection or withdrawal

♦ Depression

Guidelines for Discussion

Bearing in mind the preceding "red flags," the following are some guidelines for conducting classroom discussions following critical incidents. In general:

♦ Conduct the discussion in a comfortable place, away from crisis-related stimuli such as visual or auditory reminders, TV or radio announcements, emergency vehicle traffic, etc.

♦ Maintain calm both personally and within the group. The leader's calm demeanor models that behavior for students and encourages trust. The implicit message is "It's okay."

♦ Be aware of your own reactions and limits. If, as discussion leader, you are unable to handle the situation, someone else should take over.

♦ Observe your students' behavior for congruency with their speech. While a child may say one thing, his or her body language may be saying something quite different and more important.

- Validate students' feelings. While strong feelings often lie just below the surface, and students should not be encouraged to act them out during a discussion, those feelings should be acknowledged. Convey the message: "It's normal to have unusual and strong feelings during times like this."

- Listen with attention, focus, and empathy. Use gentle probes for elaboration and increasingly focused questions when necessary. Maintain good eye contact, and be aware of the messages posture can send out.

- Show confidence, trust, and faith that the student is telling the truth as he or she sees it. Do not seek to place blame.

- Look for misplaced blame or responsibility children may place upon themselves for things that happened during the crisis. Help clarify what happened and dispel any self-blame.

- Keep a balance between support and overcontrol regarding the expression of anxiety. Without creating contagious hysteria, provide the opportunity to assist students in exploring their fears. Provide reality checks and assurance as appropriate. Observe different students' reactions and keep the discussion from becoming hurtful.

- Provide clear, accurate, and understandable information when possible. Don't contradict feelings, but do help students to understand the situation. Sometimes situations require predictable changes in routine. When such changes are fairly certain, explain what is going to happen and walk students through the process.

- Point out available resources at school and in the community; pass out fact sheets so students can take information home that they may otherwise fail to remember.

♦ Help students link up in natural support groupings. Networking for mutual support is very helpful.

> *Let students know that you are available if they need to talk to you after the discussion or at a later time.*

9

Group and Classroom Interventions

If school crisis teams are available, they may be able to do more specialized interventions with your students. These may take the form of classroom discussions (like we just outlined), classroom defusings, or classroom debriefings (described below). People who are specially trained should conduct such interventions.

Classroom defusings are typically conducted with intact groups such as classes or smaller groups of children who have been impacted together by a critical incident. Defusings are provided when the critical incident is over and before students leave for home. A defusing is a small group meeting that marks the event as serious, allows the supervising adult (such as the teacher) to maintain classroom control, and sets the stage for future group processing of the event.

Sometimes crisis-response-team personnel are available for conducting more structured group discussions called *classroom debriefings*. Debriefings can be formal or informal and are usually led by crisis-response personnel or by teachers in collaboration with crisis-response-team members. Classroom debriefings aim at reestablishing classroom control by opening a brief, structured discussion of the event within the group. Additional goals are to approximate the aims of individual crisis intervention, assess students' need for further intervention, and reduce the level of reaction to the incident on both the individual and group levels.

Trained crisis-team members may also conduct follow-up discussions and activities in-class in the months following the incident.

(Defusing and debriefing protocols are adapted from George Everly and Jeffrey Mitchell's *Critical Incident Stress Management* [Chevron Press, 1999], and elaborated in Kendall Johnson's *School Crisis Management* [Hunter House Publishers, 2000].)

10

~~mm~~

Talking with Children about War, Terror, and Disaster

Our world is changing rapidly. Large-scale disasters such as hurricanes, earthquakes, and tornadoes now seem almost routine compared to the increasing prevalence of war, terrorist attacks, and mass murder. Increasingly, we face incidents that are overwhelming.

Large-scale incidents often create climates of fear, anger, and confusion in homes throughout the community. A sense of emergency may stalk the community, and the media may project heightened vulnerability and hysteria. Home cannot be assumed to be a refuge of safety or support. Parents are as likely as anyone to be adversely impacted by these events, and their parenting may be affected accordingly.

Children need to talk about crisis. War, terror, and disaster confuse and scare children, and talking with a teacher or another adult can help. Use the techniques of individual conferencing and classroom discussion to address issues of children's perceptions and understanding of the events, their reactions, and ways they can cope. Keep in mind the following considerations:

- Stay politically neutral.

- Don't use the classroom as a forum for your own opinions.

- While it is important to let students express their opinions and feelings, it is also important to maintain enough structure to protect students from heated discussions that can set them up for repercussions later.

- Begin where they are. Start with what they know, what they think they know, and what they are feeling.

- Clarify misunderstandings, but also allow students to think things out for themselves.

- Know that feelings may run high both in the classroom and at home.

- Understand that what goes on in the classroom may carry over into the larger campus and the community.

- Make sure you keep the theme of war, terror, or disaster balanced with other topics; students need relief from constant reminders of the crisis.

11

What *Not* to Do

It is a myth that any interaction is preferable to no interaction following a crisis. After a critical incident children are likely to be highly impressionable and emotionally vulnerable. Careless messages, heavy judgments, and bad advice can leave a lasting impression. Such bad medicine can amount to retraumatization.

The following types of interaction should be *avoided* when talking with a student who has undergone a critical incident:

♦ **Making false promises.** Do not tell the individual or group things you are actually unsure of, or that are untrue. If you are unsure of something, tell them, "I'm not sure, but I will find out for you." Do not say, "Everything is going to be all right!" unless you have some way of knowing that to be true.

♦ **Falling apart.** It's all right to shed some tears in empathy with another person, but when interacting with a child who's in a critical situation it is essential to remain in emotional control. Don't fall apart or react with excessive emotion, because that sends the message that you can't be trusted with difficult information. The student has enough to cope with; he or she does not need to be forced to take care of your emotional problems as well.

+ **Casting judgment.** Facial expression, body language, inferences, and questions can communicate judgments. Even
  "Why did you take so long to come to me?" signals an
  implied judgment that can be more than a vulnerable student can handle. Focus on the person, not upon what's
  "right."

+ **Conducting inquisitions.** Don't play detective, searching
  for information with which to hang suspected perpetrators.
  Pushing for information prematurely simply uses the victim
  for purposes other than helping him deal with his reactions.
  Such inquisition will only drive the student away or make
  things worse. Instead, assist the student in revealing what he
  feels is necessary. Work with that. Follow your state and district policies—and the dictates of your conscience—in
  reporting child abuse or endangerment.

DON'T

Make false promises

Fall apart

Cast judgment

Conduct an inquisition

Avoid mandated reporting

12

mmm

Dealing with
Distraught Parents

When children are threatened, parents react. Sometimes their reactions are appropriate and sometimes not. Parents may unwittingly make situations worse, further victimize their children, and perpetrate new emergencies through misguided or poorly controlled behavior.

Sometimes the crisis is something that happened at school or in the community. If it happened at school, the teacher is often perceived as the source for redress or as the cause of the crisis. If it happened at home, the parent may feel that the teacher has all the answers, or can magically make the trouble go away. Whatever its origin, crisis can have a destabilizing effect on the family and can undermine family functioning—which in turn can make the crisis worse.

A common reaction of parents in crisis is to displace their fear and anger on the classroom teacher. Blaming, criticizing, belittling, or even verbal attack are forms of displaced anger and frustration. It is very difficult to be supportive and calm with parents who have lost control of their feelings and behavior.

Here's what you can do:

+ **Understand their fears.** No one put an owner's manual in the parents' hands when they had their child. There are no unimpeachable directions about how to parent well in all circumstances. Most parents care deeply about their children and worry about whether they are doing well by their children. When their children get hurt, they get upset as much by their own lack of knowledge and ability as by the situation that hurt the child.

♦ **Know their need to express anger and frustration as well as their tendency to displace it.** In all likelihood, you are not the target. If you are, you're probably the wrong one. Begin by listening, and let them know they are heard.

♦ **Act as an agent of calm.** Whether or not they believe it to be so, most parents *want* the teacher to be a source of stability and calm in their child's life. By virtue of your position alone, you will be a lightning rod for parental uncertainty. Understanding this fact can help you see that it is not you as you that attracts the energy; rather it is you as Teacher. Let that energy continue right past you. Respond calmly, knowing that your calm is what they came for.

♦ **Provide simple information that can guide action.** If you understand what underlies the crisis, share that knowledge in simple form. If there are steps parents can take to support or guide their children, pass them along. Where resources exist, redirect them to those resources. When you don't understand things, or don't know what to do, share that too. Take it as a call to collaborative searching. A good answer is always: "I don't know. Let's find out."

♦ **Remember that it is their problem, not yours.** Ultimately the problems of raising children rest in the hands of those raising them. It may "take a village," and you may be a central figure in that village, but in the end the parents really have the responsibility. You can listen, empathize, make suggestions, and give support, but it's still their problem, not yours. As much as they would like to dump the problem into your lap, they can't, and you cannot let them.

♦ **Protect yourself.** Parents cannot yell at you or blame you. They cannot demand that you fix the situation or their child if the situation they face is out of your control. If you feel assaulted by a parent, go to your administrator. One of your administrator's responsibilities is to protect you so you can do your job. If your administrator cannot protect you, talk to your collective bargaining agency and seek assistance. Talk to other teachers about your situation and ask for their assistance. Follow the suggestions for self-care in this booklet.

13

Understanding Administrator Stress

In an ideal world, administrators support teachers. The administrator recognizes that the primary work of the school takes place with children in the classroom, and that the prime mover is the teacher. The administrator is a support person, a behind-the-scenes facilitator who leads the cheers, parts the troubled waters, and protects the classroom process.

Unfortunately, things aren't always ideal, particularly during times of crisis. Administrators often prove themselves all too human and sometimes complicate the efforts of teachers to manage classroom crises effectively and professionally. When this happens, there are a few things to keep in mind that will help you get the leadership you need.

Remember that—organizationally—the administrator is the most vulnerable to postcrisis repercussions. School boards and superintendents often target principals as the fall guys when things go wrong. This may result in high stress levels and affect the principal's ability to think through the situation and respond to you supportively.

The administrator's initial reaction may be to want to deny or minimize the situation. Administrators sometimes project the same message as the Wizard of Oz in the Broadway musical *The Wiz:*

"Whatever you do, don't you bring me no bad news!" It is your responsibility to make known the implications of the situation as you see it. If you need immediate assistance at the classroom level, or in dealing with parents or others from the outside, be specific in your requests.

Let the administrator know that you appreciate the complication presented to him or her by the problem. Use phrases like "I understand that...," "It looks like we have to...," and "Would you like me to...?" Adopt a calming tone of voice. Set the stage for positive interchange.

Where possible, approach the problem collaboratively. Avoid projecting a victim or dependent image; use calming language and posture. Lend strength to the administrator while seeking positive approaches.

Be open in supplying contextual background information where it might be helpful in understanding the situation fully. Make it clear when you are presenting background information, and distinguish between what you have seen, the sense you make of it, and what you have heard from others.

Be aware of your own rights and needs in the situation, and communicate them directly. If you can see where specific types of support would help you to do your job, ask for them. If you need extra time, space, or psychological support, don't be afraid to ask.

Consult with your collective bargaining representative or attorney if you feel you are being treated unfairly or are being inadequately protected by your school administrator or the district administration.

14

mm

Your Own Reaction

While we would like to feel competent in all things and walk through turmoil and difficulty unscathed, that is rarely the case. Most of us look back at our "finest hours" and either laugh or cry at how we felt at the time. It is normal to feel only marginally competent, in control, and effective during crisis. Usually we decide only later that we really managed the situation fairly well.

Crises in the classroom tend to engender unsettling feelings in staff members. Here are some common types of reactions to both individual and group crisis-management situations:

- **Fear over liabilities.** Many professionals facing crisis situations suddenly become aware of their professional vulnerability. Specific fears over legal responsibilities and liabilities are legitimately raised.

- **Guilt.** Professionals commonly feel guilt over failing to see the signs of crisis sooner or failing to act sooner than they did. Of all professional groups, teachers seem to be the most prone to guilt.

- **Feelings of inadequacy.** When confronted with catastrophic situations, staff members often feel that they can do little to "fix" the pain. The expectation that "I should be able to fix it" leads to feelings of helplessness.

- **Anger.** Feelings of anger and rage are often the result of dealing with children who have been victimized by adults. Related to this feeling is rage over the more general human condition that is fraught with unjust and unwarranted pain.

- **Desire to protect.** Listening to a child's pain and hearing about the unfortunate situations he's endured often creates a desire to provide 100 percent protection for the child 100 percent of the time. Obviously this cannot be, and usually the damage has already occurred. This creates further frustration for the teacher.

- **Distrust.** Distrust of the home situation, the law-enforcement system, and the helping system are natural. This is further fed by the "What Ifs." What if the perpetrator gets out; what if the police don't catch him; what if he gets a light sentence; what if the parents take it out on the child; what if it happens again; what if…?

- **Reemergence of old personal issues.** Often the student's critical incident or life situation parallels your own past or present. While this can create shared experience, rapport, and understanding, it can also create discomfort, pain, and significant distraction. The adult's unfinished business can interfere with his or her focus on the student and can drain away needed energy.

- **Vulnerability later.** Overinvolvement, unfinished business, or the intensity of the situation can leave the adult in great emotional turmoil, needfulness, and self-doubt later. Now is the time to find a support person and take care of yourself.

BOTTOM LINE

If you can't focus on the student because of your own emotional involvement, GET HELP in dealing with the student, and take care of yourself.

15

mm

Self-Care

Dealing with classroom crisis places teachers in jeopardy. *Direct* exposure to grotesque sensory stimuli can leave difficult memories and unsettling feelings. *Indirect* exposure to a student's suffering can have the same effect. This occurs through a combination of self-produced imagery, personal involvement with the student, and a sense of responsibility. As a result, in the aftermath of an overwhelming event, teachers are often left not only with feelings of inadequacy or guilt, but possibly also with their own symptoms of distress.

It is helpful to remember that individuals who weren't actually present at the event—whether they be teachers or students—experience not only what they see and hear, but also what they imagine and fear. And the images we create in our minds are often more powerful than direct exposure to a critical incident.

It is also helpful to remember that teachers bring their own fears, needs, self-doubts, guilt, and shame to the whole situation. At the same time, however, the teacher remains responsible for students' safety, no matter how much of his or her own "stuff" the teacher brings to the mix.

Teacher Protection

Teachers can do much to protect themselves before, during, and after classroom crisis. But in order to do so, taking steps toward proactive self-care is essential. Following the strategies outlined below will buffer the personal effects of difficult situations.

◇ Prior to a Crisis

♦ **Build awareness of your personal vulnerability and limitations.** Learn about areas where you may be especially sensitive because of prior crises in your life. Be honest with yourself about what kinds of situations you are good at handling, and what kinds of situations you need help with.

♦ **Realize your need for support; know whom to turn to after an incident.** Before a critical event happens, think about what sorts of assistance you could use in different kinds of crisis situations and who might be willing to provide it to you. Consider developing a list of people you trust and could talk to when things become difficult. Besides the crisis-response-team personnel that your school or district may make available to you, trusted coworkers, friends, and family members can help you keep perspective and can point out things you may have failed to consider.

♦ **Plan for routine self-care following critical incidents.** Make a list of the things that keep you healthy. Whether it be exercise, diet, or spiritual activity, plan ways to maintain that care system after an emergency.

♦ **Keep your support system in place.** Crisis uses up resources. Remind yourself who is available that can help you, and reach out to them. If you think you might need them later, let them know so they can be aware of your need.

♦ **Do ongoing work on personal issues that leave you vulnerable.** Everybody has personal issues that tend to get worse during periods of stress. Keep working on them now.

♦ **Set limits on demands from others and from yourself.**
As a normal human being, you have limits on your time,
energy, and resources. During crisis your limits are stretched
even thinner. Learn skills now in setting limits so you won't
let others leave you totally drained after a crisis.

♦ **Learn ahead of time about the systems that are in
place in your school for dealing with different kinds
of crisis.** Different kinds of emergencies require different
responses—a fire, for example, requires a separate set of
responses than that needed for a bomb threat. The more
familiarity you have with the specific requirements of your
school for dealing with each scenario, the greater will be
your ability to respond effectively.

◇ **During Classroom Crisis**

♦ Maintain a level of discipline and control that you are comfortable with.

♦ Monitor your own response level on the seven-point scale
outlined in the section "Managing Behavior During Emergencies." This will help you assess the situation and stay
within the response range where you can be most effective.

♦ Make sure that your evaluation of the situation isn't colored
by your own personal issues or fears.

♦ Utilize support as much as possible.

♦ Let others help or even take over when necessary.

♦ So that you can remain effective as you help others, use
the techniques for handling agitation and shutdown on
yourself, if necessary. See below for how to apply these tools
to yourself.

Self-Care for Agitation

Begin with a self-assessment. Ask yourself: Am I agitated?

Some specific questions to consider include:

♦ Is this situation threatening? How much actual threat is there?

♦ Is the threat from outside me or inside me?

♦ What is my reaction level (on the seven-point scale)?

♦ Do I feel panic, rage, or hysteria?

♦ What is my body telling me?

♦ Does time seem to be slowing down?

♦ How are others acting and reacting?

♦ What might they see that I don't?

♦ Can I ask them?

♦ What evidence could I look for to confirm my feelings and reactions?

Next, if necessary, utilize the tools outlined in "Managing Behavior During Emergencies." These are summarized in the table below.

Self-Care Actions for Agitation	
Tool	**How to use it**
Focus	Use soothing and calming self-talk; talk to others
Imagery, expectations	Visualize a safe place; visualize positive actions and outcomes

Self-Care Actions for Agitation (cont'd.)	
Tool	**How to use it**
Attend to the present	Ignore memories and imagination; focus on the present
Breath	Initiate four-count breathing
Relaxation	Sit down; change scenery
Activity	Stretch; take a relaxing walk; do a calming ritual
Direction	Find something useful to do; find support and assistance

Self-Care for Shutdown

Ask yourself: Am I shutting down?

Some specific questions to consider include:

♦ Do things seem to be slipping out of control and beyond my understanding?

♦ Am I beginning to feel that things just don't seem to matter?

♦ What is my reaction level (on the seven-point scale)?

♦ Am I aware of my body?

♦ Do others seem agitated compared to me?

♦ Does time seem to be going too fast?

♦ Are people talking loudly at me, or getting in my face?

♦ What might they be seeing that I don't?

Next, if necessary, utilize the tools outlined in "Managing Behavior During Emergencies." These are summarized in the table below.

Self-Care Actions for Shutdown	
Tool	**How to use it**
Focus	Use positive, empowering self-talk; speak to others
Imagery, expectations	Visualize positive actions and successful outcomes
Attend to the present	Ignore memories and imagination; focus on the present
Breath	Initiate quick breaths
Arousal	Get up and move; shake it off
Relaxation	Sit down; change scenery
Activity	Take a power walk; exercise; do a strengthening ritual
Direction	Find something useful to do; find support and assistance

Following a Crisis

Use the following strategies to help yourself heal in the aftermath of a classroom crisis:

+ Review the incident with another professional, either a teacher or administrator.

+ Monitor your emotional reactions, thoughts, sleep, and imagery.

- Debrief according to your self-care plan. Talk to others. Reach out for their input as to how things are going and what you need.

- Eat, sleep, and exercise moderately and well; don't overextend yourself.

- Work at putting the incident into narrative format by writing and telling others about it.

- Find creative expression for deep processing of your experience at the time and later.

- Process the experience with a mental-health professional.

- Understand and appreciate your own need for acknowledgement and nurture; seek it out.

Handling a student crisis is usually a crisis for the teachers as well! Routines are disrupted, different management skills are called for, and emotions are draining. Even more stressful, student crises are rarely "fixable." There are usually no clear resolutions; worse, there are often no clear criteria for determining what is or is not successful intervention. Only with experience can professionals walk away from interventions feeling "Yes, that felt good" or "No, that really did not work out." There are few standards, few norms, and few evaluation systems to tell us how we have done.

Over the Long Haul

Crisis means stress. Stress works in an interactive cycle, with our reaction to stressful situations compounding the situation itself, creating more stress. Stress management involves some long-range planning that focuses upon our expectations, our manner of interpreting situations, and an evaluation of the way our behavior makes situations worse or better.

In the short run it is useful to have several brief stress-cycle-breaking techniques available. A useful strategy is to plan time slots of five to ten minutes during the day when you can be by yourself. Use a relaxation technique such as brief meditation, self-hypnosis, or simple stretching. Follow this by sharing your reactions to the incident with someone else prior to going home.

Crises that feel like "the straw that broke the camel's back" often trigger larger personal stress reactions. Everyone experiences stress differently, but there are four general areas of impact: physical, psychological, family, and work. The type of impact experienced can provide clues to working out an effective management plan.

◈ Physical

Some people react to stress primarily physically. They suffer from fatigue, headaches, colds and flu, weight problems, or sleep disturbances. Management plans could include a physical exam, eating well, appropriate exercise, and a regular sleep schedule. In addition, it is important to become familiar with the body's early warning signs that stress is building up, so that rest can be scheduled, or necessary changes made.

◈ Psychological

Some people react to stress psychologically. Depression, anxiety, overidentification with students, frustration and anger, and substance abuse can be manifestations of stress. It is important to remember that the meaning of crisis events for us—and our reactions to them—stems from our underlying personal issues. Management plans could include good consultation—whether that be with a trusted friend, a professional, or a support group—where feelings can be shared and perspectives explored.

◇ Family

Some people react by letting family relationships deteriorate. Strained spouse or child relationships, decreased affection, the intrusion of job tensions, no time for friends—each of these signals a need for reevaluation. Management plans could include creation of stronger boundaries between work and home, the development of additional support outside both work and family, exposure to other, less conflict-ridden children than those encountered at work, and scheduling time to include family activities.

◇ Work/Teaching

Finally, some people react by letting the stress affect their teaching. Triggered by unrealistic expectations and actual job difficulties, burnout signs can include feelings of being overloaded, overwhelmed, overinvolved, and overidentified with students or with the job. In addition, burnout signs can include role reversal and ambiguity, accidents, inability to detach, decreased job satisfaction, and feelings of being in a career trap. Management plans could include:

- taking time off
- developing support outside both job and home
- reexamining expectations and priorities
- establishing a team approach
- reconsidering work roles
- exploring a change of assignment or duties
- determining whether to take a more assertive posture with either staff or students
- exploring personal issues that affect the job
- consulting with a mentor, advisor, counselor, or therapist regarding professional issues

Conclusion

The classroom experience is vitally important in the lives of children, particularly when things go wrong. And a sense of stability is, in turn, vital to the life of the classroom. The methods outlined in this book provide you with the tools you will need to stabilize your classroom and yourself during emergencies and crises. Remember that you do not have to do everything in this book, nor do you have to do things perfectly, to have an enormously stabilizing effect. Like the old poker saying: It isn't so much the hand you're dealt, but how you play it that counts. A few right actions undertaken by a savvy teacher can turn chaos back into order—and important life lessons can be learned along the way!

Resources

For further information about school crisis, consult my books:

Trauma in the Lives of Children: Crisis and Stress Management Techniques for Counselors, Teachers, and Other Professionals (Alameda, CA: Hunter House Publishers, 1989)

School Crisis Management: A Hands-On Guide to Training Crisis-Response Teams, Second Edition (Alameda, CA: Hunter House Publishers, 2000).

State Emergency Services

Each state has an office of emergency services. Directions about how to contact your state's emergency agency can be found on the website of the Federal Emergency Management Agency's Global Emergency Management System:

www.fema.gov/gems/g_cats1.jsp?group1=102&groupName=Sta te+Emergency+Management+Agencies+%28U.S.A.%29

Each of the state emergency offices operates a website that provides regional information as well as contacts to local and county-level emergency services.

Centers for Disease Control and Prevention (CDC)

Information specific to biological, radiological, and chemical threats can be found at the Centers for Disease Control and Prevention (part of the U.S. Department of Health and Human Services). The CDC provides preparedness information, epidemiological updates, directions for emergency response, and links to other resources:

Phone: (404) 639-3311
Main website: www.bt.cdc.gov

Further, the CDC operates an emergency website titled "What to Do in an Emergency":

www.bt.cdc.gov/emcontact/index.asp

The CDC also offers a website that provides contact information for state and local health departments as well as a wide variety of other health- and emergency-related agencies and organizations:

www.cdc.gov/other.htm#states

Disaster Preparedness

Because phone lines and websites are likely to be overloaded in the event of emergency, it is a good idea to access and download important information beforehand. Critical information should be stored in hard copy.

The Federal Emergency Management Agency offers a website for general disaster information, including preparedness, response, and recovery:

www.fema.gov/library/dizandemer.shtm

Links to other federal emergency agencies can be found at:

http://ndms.dhhs.gov/Links/Federal_Links/federal_links.html

Practical information about what to do in biological, radiological, or chemical emergencies is downloadable from the CDC websites listed in the section above.

Mental Health

For information on mental-health issues, contact the National Institute of Mental Health:

Phone: (301) 443-4513
Websites: www.nimh.nih.gov/publicat/index.cfm

and

www.nimh.nih.gov/publicat/childmenu.cfm

Children

A general health website for children is sponsored by the Office of Disease Prevention and Health Promotion (part of the U.S. Department of Health and Human Services):

www.healthfinder.gov/kids

Local Resources

If the emergency is large-scale and located in your area, radio stations will broadcast the locations of public relief shelters. Information about this can be accessed through the American Red Cross.

Your school district and community offer a number of other resources for information and services. Prior to an emergency, you can search out these resources and write down contact information below:

Name, program, or organization	Contact information
On my site:	

Name, program, or organization	Contact information

In the school district:

Name, program, or organization	Contact information

In my community:

Notes:

Notes: